essentials

Springer essentials

Springer essentials provide up-to-date knowledge in a concentrated form. They aim to deliver the essence of what counts as "state-of-the-art" in the current academic discussion or in practice. With their quick, uncomplicated and comprehensible information, essentials provide:

- an introduction to a current issue within your field of expertise
- an introduction to a new topic of interest
- an insight, in order to be able to join in the discussion on a particular topic

Available in electronic and printed format, the books present expert knowledge from Springer specialist authors in a compact form. They are particularly suitable for use as eBooks on tablet PCs, eBook readers and smartphones. *Springer essentials* form modules of knowledge from the areas economics, social sciences and humanities, technology and natural sciences, as well as from medicine, psychology and health professions, written by renowned Springer-authors across many disciplines.

More information about this series at http://www.springer.com/series/16761

John G. Haas

COVID-19 and Psychology

People and Society in Times of Pandemic

 Springer

John G. Haas
St. Pölten University of Applied Sciences
St. Pölten, Austria

ISSN 2197-6708   ISSN 2197-6716   (electronic)
essentials
ISSN 2731-3107   ISSN 2731-3115   (electronic)
Springer essentials
ISBN 978-3-658-34892-2   ISBN 978-3-658-34893-9   (eBook)
https://doi.org/10.1007/978-3-658-34893-9

Responsible Editor: Joachim Coch
This Springer imprint is published by the registered company Springer Fachmedien Wiesbaden
GmbH part of Springer Nature.
The registered company address is: Abraham-Lincoln-Str. 46, 65189 Wiesbaden, Germany

What You Can Find in This *essential*

- What role the human psyche plays in epidemics and pandemics.
- How the COVID-19 pandemic is affecting people's psyches.
- What behaviors people exhibit in the context of the COVID-19 pandemic.
- How to manage the COVID-19 pandemic well from a psychological perspective.

Preface to the International Edition

"Like an invasion of hostile space aliens, COVID-19 is attacking the human species and won't negotiate with anyone. It cares not of your nationality, ideology, politics, or religion. This enemy of us all requires a cooperative global effort to combat, guided by the methods and tools of science and not by magical thinking." Neil deGrasse Tyson (2020), US astrophysicist.

When the World Health Organization (WHO) defined a priority list of global health emergencies in 2018, disease X topped the list. Disease X was not an actual disease, but a placeholder for a pandemic that would have a massive impact on humanity. Looking at that list today, the COVID-19 pandemic has taken the place of that placeholder.

When the first reports of a newly outbreaked flu epidemic in China circulated at the end of December 2019, the global public took little notice. As a result, rumors of a strikingly high number of infected people ran rampant on Chinese social media until the third week of January 2020, when a turnaround occurred in Western media, fueled by initial studies and reports. The result was an almost unmanageable abundance of an estimated nine billion media reports, as well as uncounted posts on social media and a rapidly growing number of scientific studies.

On March 11, 2020, the COVID-19 epidemic in China was finally officially upgraded to a global pandemic by the Director-General of WHO, Dr. Tedros Adhanom Ghebreyesus, due to the rapid increase in the number of cases in an increasing number of countries outside China. As of August 2021, 210 million cases and more than 4.3 million deaths have now been officially recorded worldwide, whereas the WHO claims that the true number might include 1.2 million more deaths than officially reported in 2020.

Currently, the majority of media reports, but also research, is still concerned with the effects on physical health, which may make the role of the human psyche seem secondary. However, since psychological aspects play an equally important role in the sense of a holistic view and a successful coping with the pandemic, this book is dedicated to this area on the basis of current scientific findings.

It can already be said that the COVID-19 pandemic has left deep scars on all levels of human activity and sentiment and will go down in history. As far as the best possible management of the situation is concerned, it is not only up to governments, experts, health systems and professionals, but ultimately up to each individual to act responsibly. Understanding the psychological background and the social context is of essential benefit in this regard.

Vienna, Austria   John G. Haas
in August 2021

Acknowledgements

Ben John & Marina – for your love and your support

Advice of Abu Jafar Ahmad Ibn Khatimah on Warding Off and Coping with the Plague (From the Year 1349)

"It is most expedient to create joy, serenity, relaxation, and hope. One should attempt to create them with permitted means as often as possible. One should seek out agreeable, dear, and charming company. [...] Let me warn of disparaging others, especially when it is accompanied by sadness. [...] Avoid all excitement, all anger and horror, in short, everything which causes emotion."

Probably the first surviving advice on coping psychologically with a pandemic.

Contents

About the Author

John G. Haas[1] is working as a lecturer at two Austrian Universities for Applied Science since 2013 and teaches Psychology, Data Science and Future Studies. Previously, he worked for 15 years in online agencies (most recently as Creative Director). In 2014, he laid the foundation for a psychosocial online service with Europe's first women's aid app "fem:help", which was used by the Republic of Austria. In 2004 he developed the European Communication Certificate (Eco-C), a qualification programme for job seekers that is still widely used by the Austrian state employment office. He is currently working on projects in the fields of digital health and infodemiology and regularly gives lectures and webinars on psychological topics.

For more content on COVID-19 and psychology, visit the companion website to the book at www.min dster.at/covid-19-and-psychology

---

[1] John G. Haas, graduate psychologist, entrepreneur and innovator.

Epidemics and Pandemics—Why They Occur and How They Are Combated

Infectious diseases and their health, economic and social consequences have accompanied mankind since the beginning of time. Moreover, they have left their mark on the cultural and historical heritage of mankind, with some diseases such as the plague or cholera becoming a symbol of a fateful event and of illness, suffering and death. In the past, it was often overlooked that psychological factors play an essential role in both the emergence and the control of epidemics and pandemics.

1.1 What is a Pandemic?

Although scientists have not been able to agree on a binding definition of a pandemic, there is no doubt about its main characteristics. Leading researchers suggest the following factors, when present, can be considered a pandemic. These are wide geographic extension, disease movement, high attack rates and explosiveness, minimal population immunity, novelty, infectiousness, contagiousness and severity of the disease (Morens et al., 2009).

1.2 Why Do Epidemics and Pandemics Occur?

The causes of the emergence and spread of infectious diseases are diverse and interconnected. A recent presentation of the most important factors in the emergence and spread of infectious diseases clearly shows that the majority are a direct or indirect consequence of human actions and are thus psychologically determined (Morens et al., 2008).

© Springer Fachmedien Wiesbaden GmbH, part of Springer Nature 2021
J. G. Haas, *COVID-19 and Psychology,* essentials,
https://doi.org/10.1007/978-3-658-34893-9_1

13 Factors that Give Rise to Epidemics and Pandemics

1. International trade and commerce
2. Human demographics and behaviour
3. Human susceptibility to infection
4. Poverty and social inequality
5. War and famine
6. Breakdown of public-health measures
7. Technology and industry
8. Changing ecosystems
9. Climate and weather
10. Intent to harm
11. Lack of political will
12. Microbial adaptation and change
13. Economic development and land use

See also Table 1.1 for an allocation of factors to historically relevant epidemics and pandemics.

Table 1.1   Historically relevant epidemics and pandemics and their contributing factors

Years	Emerging disease	Estimated number of human deaths	Disease factors
430–426 BC	Plague of Athens	40,000	2, 5, 7, 9, 11
1347+	Black Death	~50 million	2, 5, 6, 7, 8, 10, 11, 13
1494–1499	French pox (Syphilis)	>50,000	1, 2, 5, 7, 11
1520–1521	Hueyzahuatl (Smallpox)	3.5 million	2, 7, 10, 11, 13
1793–1798	The American plague	~25,000	2, 3, 4, 5, 6, 7, 8, 9, 10, 12
1832	Second cholera pandemic, Paris	~18,000	3, 5, 7, 8, 10
1918–1919	Spanish influenza	~50+ million	1, 2, 5, 7, 11
1981+	AIDS pandemic	25+ million	1, 2, 4, 5, 7, 8, 9, 10, 12
2020+	COVID-19 pandemic	4.3 million	1, 2, 3, 4, 6, 8, 9, 11, 12, 13[a]

[a]in the author's assessment

If we consider infectious diseases in terms of their diverse and interconnected causes, a systemic context emerges which, taken together, represents a challenge for humankind which, in extreme cases, can rapidly develop into a global threat (Morens et al., 2008) Table 1.1.

For this reason, the global community is called upon not only in times of a pandemic to recognize the causes and dynamics of infectious diseases, but also to act in a forward-looking, cooperative and goal-oriented manner in the interest of a successful human existence.

1.3 How Epidemics and Pandemics Are Combated

In the context of combating an epidemic or pandemic, a distinction is made between three types of measures (interventions). These are vaccinations, pharmaceutical interventions and nonpharmaceutical interventions (NPIs). As long as vaccinations are not available, NPIs are the most effective measures.

What are nonpharmaceutical interventions?
Nonpharmaceutical interventions are all methods used to combat epidemics and pandemics without the need for medical treatment.

The US Centers for Disease Control and Prevention (CDC) classify nonpharmaceutical interventions in the context of an epidemic or pandemic into three groups (Table 1.2).

Nonpharmaceutical interventions have proven effective many times in the past and were used during the H1N1 (swine flu) pandemic in 2009. A review of 4579 interventions in the context of the COVID-19 pandemic in 76 regions worldwide found that, while there is no single effective intervention, the combination of multiple interventions proved to be very effective. Furthermore, a clear ranking of intervention or measure areas can be identified (Haug et al., 2020).

Table 1.2 Classification of nonpharmaceutical interventions (NPIs)

Personal NPIs	Respiratory hygiene, hand hygiene, social hygiene
Community NPIs	"Social distancing", wearing of mouth-nose protection masks, travel restrictions, closures, restrictions on the number of people, risk communication
Environmental NPIs	Regular cleaning of surfaces of frequently touched objects, infrastructural measures

The 4 main nonpharmaceutical interventions in COVID-19

- Spatial distancing ("social distancing")
- Healthcare and public health capacity
- Travel restrictions
- Risk communication

Since some measures involve a restriction of individual freedom, albeit in favour of a socially overriding objective, they are often perceived as unpleasant, burdensome, restrictive or even threatening, which makes compliance with them difficult or can cause psychological stress.

Conclusion

- Infectious diseases have accompanied mankind since the beginning and have sometimes assumed threatening proportions.
- The many causes of epidemics and pandemics together form a complex system, most of which have a psychological background.
- Epidemics and pandemics can in principle be well controlled by a combination of nonpharmaceutical interventions and medical measures.

The Human Psyche – A Brief Consideration

2

"The soul is a vast domain." Arthur Schnitzler (1911)

The word psyche comes from ancient Greek and originally meant "breath" or "breeze" and was used in ancient Greece in a broader sense to describe the whole person, up to and including the most valuable thing of all.

Used in today's sense, psyche refers to the unique totality of all mental or non-physical characteristics and abilities of a person. These include attention, perception, emotion, motivation, and cognition (i.e., all "mental" abilities such as planning, thinking, and learning). Unlike the concept of soul, the concept of psyche does not include transcendent elements.

2.1 The Human Being as a Biopsychosocial Unit

Since a one-dimensional view of the human being does not do justice to it, this must take place on as broad a basis as possible in order to represent the uniqueness, diversity and complexity of the "phenomenon" of the human being in the best possible way.

For this reason, the biopsychosocial model has become established in psychology and medicine as an aid to observation, explanation and treatment. On the basis of this model, factors and interactions that affect the experience and behavior of humans should be better explained. In addition, it can be used to illustrate mechanisms for the maintenance of health or the development of disease. (Fig. 2.1.)

Last but not least, the biopsychosocial model attempts to counteract the separate consideration of body and psyche and in this way supports a holistic view of the human being.

© Springer Fachmedien Wiesbaden GmbH, part of Springer Nature 2021
J. G. Haas, *COVID-19 and Psychology,* essentials,
https://doi.org/10.1007/978-3-658-34893-9_2

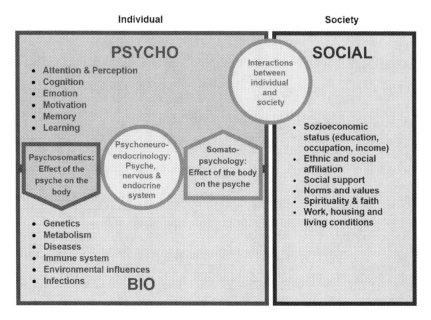

Fig. 2.1 Overview of the biopsychosocial model of the human being

2.2   What is (Mental) Health?

The World Health Organization laid the foundation for a modern view in 1946 with its definition of health, defining it in its constitution as follows: "Health is a state of complete physical, mental and social well-being and not merely the absence of disease or infirmity." This definition includes mental health as well as social well-being in addition to physical health.

2.3   How a Mental Disorder Develops and How It is Defined

In principle, one strives to keep his well-being and well-doing high through the best possible adaptation to the circumstances (own condition, social structure, environment) by creating a balance between the "inner world" and "outer world" (equilibration). Most people are usually well able to do this.

If the individual does not subjectively succeed in adaptation and equilibration, or if the resulting sensations, actions or their consequences are disadvantageous for the person concerned or the environment, we can speak of maladaptation.

Not every mental stress or external challenge automatically leads to a mental disorder, as humans have innate abilities, as well as those acquired in the course of life, which enable them to deal with stress, major changes or catastrophes (resilience). Only when the individual threshold of resilience is exceeded does the probability of the occurrence of a mental disorder increase.

As a rule, the well-being suffers first in the case of stress and thus sets a sign that there is a need for adaptation. If the individual is subsequently unable to carry out "internal" or "external" adaptive actions that are effective or increase his or her well-being, this subjective malaise can turn into a state of permanent maladaptation, which usually reduces the possibilities of further adaptation (vicious circle) and increases the risk of a mental disorder.

Definition of a mental disorder: Diagnostic and Statistical Manual of Mental Disorders (DSM), 5th edition
"A mental disorder is a syndrome characterized by clinically significant disturbance in an individual's cognition, emotion regulation, or behavior that reflects a dysfunction in the psychological, biological, or developmental processes underlying mental functioning. Mental disorders are usually associated with significant distress or disability in social, occupational, or other important activities.

An expectable or culturally approved response to a common stressor or loss, such as the death of a loved one, is not a mental disorder. Socially deviant behavior (e.g., political, religious, or sexual) and conflicts that are primarily between the individual and society are not mental disorders unless the deviance or conflict results from a dysfunction in the individual, as described above." (American Psychiatric Association, APA 2013, p. 20).

2.4   How the Psyche Expresses Itself

The presence of psychological stress or mental disorder often manifests itself in specific form on four levels and, when viewed together, provides diagnostic clues to the nature and severity of the disorder. These levels are structured in terms of the biopsychosocial model, with the psyche being represented in simplified form by two interacting components, namely emotion and cognition (Wittchen & Hoyer, 2011, p. 32).

Levels of expression of psychological stress and mental disorders

Emotional level: The way people experience and express their feelings.
Cognitive level: The way people process information, think, judge and learn.
Social level: The way people behave (motor skills, the level of social activity and the nature of interaction with other people).
Biological level: The nature of various biological parameters such as heartbeat, muscle tension or (brain) metabolism.

The subjectively perceived level of psychological distress, as well as how it is handled and expressed, depends on the individual. Thus, subjective distress ranges from weak (low psychosocial distress) to strong (high psychosocial distress).

If the psyche expresses itself in the sphere of the physical, one speaks of conversion (lat. for transformation, a turning or changing from one state to another). From the point of view of psychosomatics, the forms of expression in the sense of a "language" of the psyche are of essential diagnostic and therapeutic importance, whereby certain phenomena impressively testify to the unity of "mind and body" and thus support the assumptions of the biopsychosocial model.

Conclusion

- The biopsychosocial model tries to do justice to the diversity and uniqueness of the human being and also promotes a holistic view of the human being.
- Humans strive to ensure well-being and well-doing through equilibration and adaptation, which they usually succeed in doing.
- The sensation of psychological distress or the onset of a psychological disorder are signs that the current forms of equilibration and adaptation are not serving the individual.
- The human psyche has a wide range of possibilities for reaction and expression.

Psychological Aspects of Epidemics and Pandemics

3

"The plague was nothing; fear of the plague was much more formidable." Henri
Poincaré (1905)

3.1   Man's Fear of Infectious Diseases

Infectious diseases have always triggered negative thoughts and feelings in people,
above all fear. This fear, which is stronger than that of other diseases ("primal
fear"), can be attributed to three reasons (Pappas et al., 2009).

The three main reasons for the increased fear of infection in humans

- The character of the infectious event, as it usually occurs unnoticed and quickly,
  and becomes certain only with the appearance of symptoms.
- The role of the infected person, as he is both a victim and a vector of a disease.
- The numerous and sometimes dramatic accounts of the effects of epidemics and
  pandemics, especially with regard to the large number of people who fell ill and
  died.

A highly exaggerated fear of infections in the sense of a mental disorder is called
mysophobia. A phobia represents a special form of anxiety disorder and is characterized by an extreme fear of certain objects or situations. Affected persons often
show coping behaviour in the form of avoidance (door handles, coins, toilets, …)
or only seemingly effective protective behaviour in the form of a compulsion to
wash or clean in order to counteract an impending infection or contamination.
Because infection is transmissible, imminent and invisible, it will always pose a
potential major threat to both human body and psyche.

© Springer Fachmedien Wiesbaden GmbH, part of Springer Nature 2021
J. G. Haas, *COVID-19 and Psychology,* essentials,
https://doi.org/10.1007/978-3-658-34893-9_3

3.2   Contagion from a Psychological Perspective

The term "contagion" comes from the Latin word "contagio" (literally: "with/together" and "touch") and is used in psychology in the sense of "contagion" of behaviour (social contagion) but also of emotions (emotional contagion). Especially in the context of exceptional social situations (catastrophes, crises, epidemics/pandemics, war), contagion effects play an essential role. From experience with previous pandemics, it is known that the feeling of fear in particular spreads rapidly.

In connection with COVID-19, the rapid spread of fear, primarily mediated by the media, has often been referred to as a "second pandemic". This is worth mentioning because subjectively perceived fear has a significant influence on health behaviour and the ability to cope psychologically.

3.2.1   Social Contagion

Social contagion can be defined as the contagion of behaviour mediated by psychological mechanisms. The term was first mentioned in 1895 by Gustave Le Bon, who, in his 1895 book "The Crowd: A Study of the Popular Mind" drew a pessimistic picture of men. He described that the individual under the influence of the mass loses his ability to criticize and self-control and behaves mainly instinctively.

More recent findings put this assessment into perspective and demonstrate that although negative effects occur in exceptional social situations, positive effects such as responsible and prosocial behaviour also occur.

The image of group reactions has also changed from the view of a collective and uncontrollable mass to more complex descriptions. Thus, more sophisticated models like social identity theory (SIT) and self-categorization theory (SCT) dominate the view of groups in contemporary social science.

With regard to COVID-19, social contagion can spread and consolidate cooperative and prosocial behaviours in society. Danger in this context comes primarily from deliberately generated fear and the subsequent fear-related behaviour, as people in fear prove easier to manipulate (keywords: "culture of fear" or FUD—"Fear, uncertainty and doubt").

3.2.2 Emotional Contagion

Analogous to social contagion, emotional contagion is the contagion of emotions mediated by psychological mechanisms. From the point of view of research, the mutual and largely unconscious adaptation (mimicry) of posture, facial expression, voice and movement is primarily responsible for this.

However, emotional contagion can occur not only in direct, personal contact, but also through the media. This effect became known to a wider public in the context of the controversially discussed "Facebook study", in which emotional contagion through manipulated user timelines (contagion through emotionally positive or negative content) was impressively proven on the basis of around 700,000 users (Kramer et al., 2014).

A detrimental and concerning consequence of emotional contagion in the context of COVID-19 is that fear, in particular, spreads rapidly through media coverage and can be further amplified through social media. As a consequence, distorted risk perception, reduced health behaviour, frustration, excessive demands, reluctance and feelings of anxiety can occur.

3.3 Defense from a Psychological Point of View

3.3.1 Defense from the Perspective of Evolutionary Psychology—The Behavioural Immune System

The behavioral immune system (BIS) can be defined as a set of psychological mechanisms that enable people to protect themselves from pathogens. This goal is achieved through three interacting functional domains (Schaller and Park, 2011).

The three main functions of the human behavioral immune system

- recognition of clues to the presence of infectious agents (certain odours, visible signs of illness and behaviour) in the immediate environment,
- triggering of disease-relevant feelings (dislike, revulsion, disgust, …) and thoughts (threat, danger),
- triggering defensive behaviors (avoidance, repulsion, combat).

This evolutionary protective mechanism does not only have advantages. A serious disadvantage is that the living environment of humans has changed more rapidly than their biological development and this system reacts in the sense of "false alarms" to situations and persons from which there is no (longer) any danger. In addition, many processes of the behavioural immune system run autonomously and partly unconsciously, which makes reflection or cognitive control difficult.

Recent research suggests some controversial implications, such as that this system may foster prejudice and xenophobia (Schaller and Park, 2011).

3.3.2   Defense from the Perspective of Psychoanalysis

From a psychoanalytic perspective, a hierarchy of defense mechanisms can be established, ranging from narcissistic to immature and neurotic to mature forms. These forms are linked to specific psychopathologies and are presented here in descending adaptive order and illustrated with possible reactions in the context of the COVID-19 pandemic (Werner and Langenmayr, 2005). Table 3.1.

3.3.3   The Biopsychosocial Model of Contagion and Defence

In conclusion, from a biopsychosocial perspective, the systems of contagion and defence can be summarised and illustrated as follows. (Fig. 3.1).

3.4   The Spectrum of Mental Disorders in the Context of Epidemics and Pandemics

With regard to the range of mental disorders that develop in the context of epidemics and pandemics, the following diagnoses are frequently found in recent literature and will be cited here. Whether a disorder develops, or which disorder develops, or whether an existing disorder is exacerbated, depends, in the sense of the biopsychosocial model, on a variety of factors.

Overview of relevant disorders and behavioural factors in the context of epidemics and pandemics (including ICD-10 code)

Mental disorders in adults
Mental and behavioural disorders due to psychoactive substance use, especially alcohol (F10–F19), Schizophrenia (F20), Schizotypal disorders (F21), Delusional disorders (F22.0), Acute transient and psychotic disorders (F23), Induced delusional disorder (F24), Schizoaffective disorder (F25), Mood [affective] disorders

Table 3.1 Forms of defense and coping during epidemics and pandemics from a psychoanalytical perspective

	Narcissistic	Immature	Neurotic	Mature
Psychopathologies	Psychoses	Personality disorders, Mood (affective) disorders	Neuroses	None
Defense mechanisms	– Delusional projection – Psychotic denial of external reality – Distortion	– Projection – Schizoid fantasies – Hypochondriacal behaviour – Passive-aggressive behaviour – Acting out	– Intellectualizing – Displacement – Postponement – Reaction formation – Dissociation	– Altruism – Humor – Suppression – Anticipation – Sublimation
COVID-19 related experiences and behaviors[a]	– Denial – Delusional ideas about the origin, prevention and treatment – Overvalued ideas – Conspiracy thinking	– Depression – Violence – Pathological mistrust – Misuse – Negative expectations for the future – Accusations – Stigmatization	– Fear/Anxiety – "Hiding" of relevant aspects – sense of alienation – Criticism, doubt – Panic buying – Psychosomatic complaints – Search for alternative explanations – Overengagement – Uncertainty	– Helpfulness – Keep a sense of humour – Positive expectations for the future – Social support – Realization and development (social, artistic, spiritual, …) – Cohesion – Deferring needs

[a] relevant aspects without claim to completeness

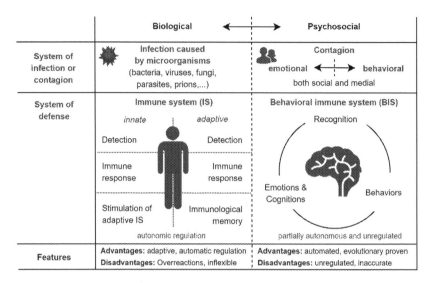

	Biological ◀──────▶	Psychosocial
System of infection or contagion	Infection caused by microorganisms (bacteria, viruses, fungi, parasites, prions,...)	Contagion emotional ◀──▶ behavioral both social and medial
System of defense	Immune system (IS) innate ┊ adaptive Detection ┊ Detection Immune response ┊ Immune response Stimulation of adaptive IS ┊ Immunological memory autonomic regulation	Behavioral immune system (BIS) Recognition Emotions & Cognitions ┊ Behaviors partially autonomous and unregulated
Features	**Advantages:** adaptive, automatic regulation **Disadvantages:** Overreactions, inflexible	**Advantages:** automated, evolutionary proven **Disadvantages:** unregulated, inaccurate

Fig. 3.1 Biopsychosocial model of contagion and defence

(F30–F39), Phobic anxiety disorders (F40), Panic disorders (F41.0), Generalized anxiety disorders (F41.1), Obsessive–compulsive disorders (F42), Acute stress reactions (F43.0), Post-traumatic stress disorders (F43.1), Adjustment disorders (F43.2), Dissociative (conversion) disorders (F44), Somatization disorders (F45.0), Hypochondriacal disorders (F45.2), Eating disorders (F50), Nonorganic sleep disorders (F51).

Mental disorders in children
Hyperkinetic disorders (F90), Conduct disorders (F91), Mixed disorders of conduct and emotions (F92), Emotional disorders with onset specific to childhood (F93), Nonorganic enuresis (F98.0).

Factors influencing health status and leading to health care utilization
Problems related to lifestyle (Z72): alcohol and tobacco use, drug use, inappropriate diet and eating habits, burnout (Z73.0), stress (Z73.3).

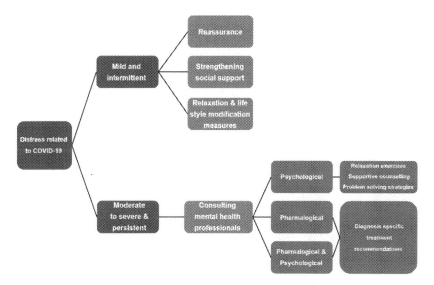

Fig. 3.2   Management of stress and mental disorders in the context of COVID-19

3.5   Management of Mental Stress and Mental Disorders in the Context of COVID-19

Depending on the nature of the stress in terms of duration and severity, the following model provides an overview of interventions (Kar et al., 2020). (Fig. 3.2.)

The main objective of all measures is to reduce psychological stress against the background that the persons concerned quickly regain the greatest possible degree of subjective well-being, self-determination and freedom of action.

3.6   Assessment of Own Psychological Well-Being

The World Health Organisation—Five Well-Being Index (WHO-5) is suitable for assessing one's own well-being in the form of a short questionnaire that provides reliable results by means of five simple questions and takes about one minute to complete. Due to its nature, this can already be used with older children and adolescents.

In addition, there are a number of other questionnaires that can be used anonymously and free of charge for self-assessment of anxiety, stress and depression or other possible problems.

In terms of interpretation, these brief procedures do a good job of assessing the extent of a problem, but they do not allow a diagnosis to be made, nor do they replace the role and services of trained mental health professionals (psychologist, psychiatrist, psychotherapist).

3.7   Resilience in Times of Epidemic and Pandemic

Resilience can be described as the ability to cope with difficult life situations or crises without lasting impairment. To this end, the resilient person draws on personal, family and social resources. In principle, a distinction is made between internal and external resilience factors.

3.8   The Role of Anxiety and Fear

The main function of the unpleasant sensations of fear or anxiety is to send a clearly perceptible signal to the individual that there is imminent dangeror threat or that a (motivational) conflict exists.

In principle, the fear of a concrete threat, can be seen as a function necessary for survival. Fear of a mass threat, such as that posed by a rapidly spreading infectious disease, is subsequently understandable, to be expected and to be regarded as trend-setting for the masses.

If an existing fear is channeled and redirected accordingly, this has the effect of reducing risk and lowering psychological stress (Shultz et al., 2016). In this context, the risk researcher Peter Sandman described the rapid spread of fear of infection as an evolutionarily meaningful process.

As known from research, an adequate level of health anxiety favours the management of pandemics, while hardly present or extremely high levels of health anxiety promote noncompliance with recommendations or reservations or even resistance.

Conclusion

- Humans exhibit an evolutionarily developed fear of infectious diseases that is designed to protect them from harm.

- Behaviour and emotions can be transmitted from person to person both in direct encounters and medially (contagion), with the transmission of fear playing the greatest role in the context of pandemics.
- Analogous to the human body, the human psyche has mechanisms of defense against infections, some of which may be detrimental to a prosperous coexistence.
- The spectrum of mental disorders in the context of epidemics and pandemics is broad, with all forms of anxiety playing a prominent role.

A Brief Psychohistory of Epidemics and Pandemics

4

"But while the nature of the distemper was such as to baffle all description, and its attacks almost too grievous for human nature to endure, it was still in the following circumstance that its difference from all ordinary disorders was most clearly shown."
Thucydides (428 BC)

Psychohistory is devoted to the study of historical events from the perspective of psychology. The first accounts of pandemics date to 1320 BC, with the first more detailed accounts coming from the Plague of Athens.

4.1   Psychohistory of the Plague of Athens

The Attic plague raged in the years 430–426 BC at the time of the Peloponnesian War in the region around Athens. The causative agent of the disease is still unclear today. However, it seems certain that the outbreak of this epidemic cost the lives of about a quarter of the population.

From a psychological point of view, the most detailed descriptions of this plague come from the historian and general Thucydides, who reports as follows (Thucydides et al., 2008)

"By far the most terrible feature in the malady was the dejection."

As for the fear of contagion and its consequences, he writes the following:

"On the one hand, if they were afraid to visit each other, they perished from neglect. [...] On the other, if they ventured to do so, death was the consequence."

© Springer Fachmedien Wiesbaden GmbH, part of Springer Nature 2021
J. G. Haas, *COVID-19 and Psychology,* essentials,
https://doi.org/10.1007/978-3-658-34893-9_4

Furthermore, Thucydides describes an emerging general indifference:

> "For as the disaster passed all bounds, men, not knowing what was to become of them,
> became utterly careless of everything, whether sacred or profane."

With regard to the development in society, the following illustration can be found:

> " [...] now did just what they pleased, coolly venturing on what they had formerly
> done only in a corner."

As for possible explanations about the origin of the plague, here is perhaps the
first conspiratorial rumor in the history of infectious diseases:

> "Suddenly falling upon Athens, it [the plague, author's note] first attacked the popu-
> lation in the Piraeus, which was the occasion of their saying that the Peloponnesians
> had poisoned the reservoirs."

4.2   Psychohistory of the Plague in the Middle Ages

The plague that struck the European continent from 1347 onwards is unanimously
described by many authors as one of the greatest catastrophes in human history.
Although expert estimates of the death rate of the "Black Death" vary between 30
and 60%, most sources agree with regard to the consequences that such massive
cuts were made in the experience and behaviour of the people of that time that
the social effects were still noticeable many centuries later. In this way, "the great
dying" or "the great pestilence", as the plague was called at the time, established
itself as a prototypical horror scenario.

   The psychosocial consequences of the occurrence of the plague were initially
characterized by panic, flight from the affected areas, and severe social disorder.
(Fig. 4.1.)

   People shunned each other and sick people were often abandoned to their fate
for fear of infection, sometimes also by their relatives. As a result, various coping
strategies became established. Some people retreated as best they could, while
others adopted an excessive and fatalistic lifestyle. Still others tried to counter
the plague through defensive measures (herbs worn on the body, magical rituals,
magic symbols).

Fig. 4.1   Contemporary depiction of social consequences of plague—woodcut "Runaways fleeing from the plague" by H. Gosson (1630)—Wellcome Collection (n.y.)

As the psychosocial stress continued, behaviors such as excessive piety and rampant forms of superstition and a "brutalization of morals" to the point of violence against others developed.

Two much-discussed extreme developments, namely the persecution of Jews and the resurgence of flagellantism, represented notable lows of this period.

Incidentally, one of the first surviving pieces of psychological advice on how to prevent the plague was penned in 1349 by Abu Jafar Ahmad Ibn Khatimah, a Muslim physician and poet who lived in Almeria, Spain. This advice seems almost prophetic in its relevance when considered in the light of contemporary research.

Advice of Abu Jafar Ahmad Ibn Khatimah in "A Description and Remedy for Escaping the Plague in the Future" (1349)

"It is most expedient to create joy, serenity, relaxation, and hope. One should attempt to create them with permitted means as often as possible. One should seek out agreeable, dear, and charming company. […] Let me warn of disparaging others, especially when it is accompanied by sadness. […] Avoid all excitement, all anger and horror, in short, everything which causes emotion." (Aberth, 2005, p. 59)

More recent studies cast doubt on the frequently portrayed extent of alienation from one another and conclude that hardship had more unifying than divisive effects in the long term.

4.3   Psychohistory of Epidemics and Pandemics in the Twentieth and Twenty-First Century

As early as 1796, a vaccine against the dreaded smallpox was developed and successfully used, while other dangerous infectious diseases (typhoid, cholera, diphtheria and rabies) could not be prevented by vaccination until the end of the nineteenth century.

As a result, many countries around the world saw widespread educational campaigns aimed at improving public hygiene in order to reduce infectious diseases. This was reflected not only in the media, but also in the efforts of a rapidly developing health industry, which extensively promoted its products.

In this way, within a few decades, the people of the early twentieth century found themselves in a world full of invisible and previously unknown pathogens, which led to a first phase of "germ panic" in the USA and Europe from about 1900 to 1940 (Tomes, 2000).

The spread of the Spanish flu (1918–1919), which drastically demonstrated the fatal consequences of infectious diseases to people and further fuelled the existing basic fear of infections, also occurred in the middle of this phase.

Many fears subsided as a result of World War II and in the face of an increasing number of vaccination programs (polio vaccination) and the eradication of smallpox (1977), until the second phase of the "germ panic" began with the discovery of the HIV virus and the resulting AIDS disease, which continues to this day (Tomes, 2000).

In popular culture, too, a large number of books and films play with the "primal fear" of infection and have taken their place in the horror genre.

Then, in the twenty-first century, it was primarily the multifaceted media reports of epidemics and pandemics such as Ebola, SARS, MERS, and the H1N1 flu that shaped people's contemporary pandemic images in the period before COVID-19.

Conclusion

- In antiquity and the Middle Ages, pandemics assumed socially threatening proportions that not only frightened people extraordinarily, but also led to panic, social disorder, and disinhibition.
- During the plague in the Middle Ages, various strategies (withdrawal, fatalistic lifestyle, defensive behaviour) were noticeable, the negative highlights being religious fanaticism and the persecution of Jews.

- One of the first pieces of psychological advice on mental coping that is still valid today was written by an Arab physician and dates back to 1349.
- Along with medical advances from the early twentieth century onwards, people were repeatedly confronted with a strong fear of infection ("germ panic").

The COVID-19 Pandemic and the Human Psyche

5

There is general consensus that the COVID-19 pandemic is an acute global health emergency that impacts the physical and mental health of large numbers of people.

5.1 The Disturbance Triad of the COVID-19 Pandemic

In principle, the range of possible mental disorders in the context of crisis situations is broad, whereby in current research a triad of stress, anxiety and depression has primarily emerged. (Fig. 5.1.)

Depending on the extent of the subjective stress, these disorders are (not only) accompanied by a restriction of the freedom of experience and behaviour of the affected individuals, which in turn has a significant impact on society's ability to cope with the pandemic as a whole ("societal resilience"). Section 8.4.

5.2 How Stress, Anxiety and Depression Develop During the COVID-19 Pandemic

Concerning the development of the mental disorders prioritized by the COVID-19 pandemic, the authors of a systematic review and meta-analysis propose a multifactorial model that includes the main factors favoring the development of stress, anxiety and depression. (Fig. 5.2.)

From the perspective of this study, these are, in short, low health literacy and low adaptive capacity, which, in combination with altered sleep and dietary habits, the influence of social media, and the strong stressors (health anxiety, stresses of quarantine, concerns about economic well-being) of the pandemic situation, favor

© Springer Fachmedien Wiesbaden GmbH, part of Springer Nature 2021   25
J. G. Haas, *COVID-19 and Psychology,* essentials,
https://doi.org/10.1007/978-3-658-34893-9_5

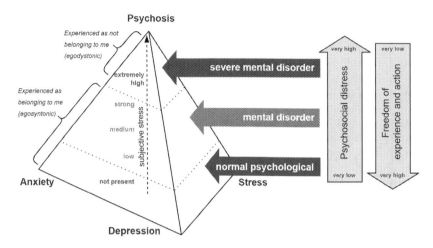

Fig. 5.1   The triad of stress, anxiety and depression as the most common mental disorders in the context of the COVID-19 pandemic

the likelihood of the development of the three disorders mentioned above (Salari et al., 2020).

5.3   Impact on the General Population

As a result of the spread of COVID-19 outside China, large-scale studies in Western countries began to yield broadly consistent findings.

A May 2020 meta-analysis reported generally reduced well-being and higher scores in anxiety and depression in the general population compared with pre-COVID-19 (Vindegaard & Benros, 2020).

The world's first systematic review and meta-analysis with data from over 100,000 people from July 2020 examined the three factors of stress, anxiety and depression in the general population. The authors found that in the period up to mid-May 2020, almost 30% of the world's population suffered from stress, while 32% suffered from anxiety and almost 34% from depressive symptoms (Salari et al., 2020).

A systematic review with data from eight countries found relatively high rates of anxiety, depression, post-traumatic stress disorder and stress in the general population (Xiong et al., 2020).

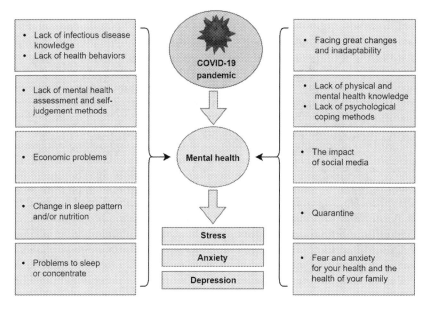

Fig. 5.2 Factors promoting stress, anxiety and depression in the context of the COVID-19 pandemic

5.4   Impact of Nonpharmaceutical Interventions

5.4.1   Isolation and Quarantine - Effective but with Unclear Consequences

According to an expert estimate as of August 2020, about one-third of the entire world population has been quarantined ("locked down") as part of the COVID-19 pandemic. The Belgian psychologist Dr. Elke van Hoof spoke in April 2020 of "this being the greatest psychological experiment of all time" with still unclear consequences for the human psyche.

How isolation and quarantine are defined
The Centers for Disease Control and Prevention (CDC) defines isolation as the separation of people with a contagious disease from other people who are not sick, while quarantine is a separation from other people and restriction of movement of people who were exposed to a contagious disease to see if they become sick.

5.4.1.1 Effects of Isolation and Quarantine on Adults

A meta-study on the psychological effects of isolation and quarantine showed that adverse effects on the human psyche are to be expected. First and foremost, confusion and anger as well as symptoms of post-traumatic stress disorder (COVID stress syndrome) were recorded. With longer quarantine periods, fear of infection, frustration and boredom as well as the feeling of insufficient information and fear of financial losses and stigmatisation also occurred (Brooks et al., 2020).

5.4.1.2 Effects of Isolation and Quarantine on Children and Adolescents

A metastudy of the effects on children and adolescents conducted during the COVID-19 pandemic reported restlessness, irritability, anxiety, increased attachment, and higher inattention associated with more time in front of screens.

In conjunction with older studies, isolation and quarantine are associated with sometimes far-reaching negative consequences for the psychological well-being of children and adolescents, as adverse effects can still occur months or years later.

To best mitigate these consequences, most authors, in agreement with the WHO, suggest intervening quickly and effectively. Among the measures mentioned are age- and developmentally appropriate teaching of facts, maintaining family routines and educational measures, maintaining a positive family climate, establishing a health-promoting lifestyle and including health promotion activities in the curriculum (Imran et al., 2020).

5.4.1.3 Recommendations for Mitigating the Effects of Isolation and Quarantine

As early as February 2020, the authors of a widely acclaimed study made recommendations for reducing psychological stress. These were to keep the period of quarantine as short as possible and to inform the affected persons as clearly as possible about the reason, the expected duration and the possibilities for psychological coping during this period (Brooks et al., 2020).

The recommendation of isolation and quarantine for as short a time as possible is supported from the perspective of psychoneuroimmunology (PNI) and from the findings of previous SARS and MERS epidemics, which indicate that massive lifestyle changes have a detrimental effect on the immune system (Kim & Su, 2020).

An opposing viewpoint is taken by a recent study that emphasizes that isolation and quarantine in the context of the current COVID-19 pandemic have not adversely affected the psyche or immune system (Milman et al., 2020).

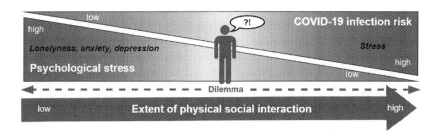

Fig. 5.3   Risk of infection by COVID-19 and increased psychological distress as a dilemma in relation to the extent of direct social contact

5.4.2   Social Distancing

Social distancing, actually more appropriately called physical distancing, means creating a safe distance between oneself and people outside one's own household to reduce the risk of transmission. In the context of the COVID-19 pandemic, public recommendations for the minimum distance vary between 1 and 2 m.

Initial research on the effects from March 2020 showed that no negative changes were noticeable when social distancing was practiced voluntarily. Most of the respondents stated that their behaviour was primarily intended to protect those around them from infection (Oosterhoff et al., 2020).

The dilemma of social contact and infection
In times of rampant infectious diseases, people are confronted with a dilemma in their social behaviour. If the person decides to isolate himself, the risk of infection decreases, but the extent of the psychological burden increases. Conversely, a person may find relief in direct social interaction, but in return is exposed to an increased risk of infection, which in turn has a psychologically stressful effect. (Fig. 5.3.)

5.4.3   Wearing of a Mouth-And-Nose-Guard ("Face Mask")

In the course of the pandemic, controversy developed in many countries about the psychological effects of wearing protective face masks (more specifically: mouth-nose covering or FFP2/N95 masks/respirators).The initial focus was on the effect of a false sense of security and the associated neglect of other means of risk reduction (social distancing, hand hygiene).

Subsequently, the beneficial social effects of mask-wearing have been highlighted by the shift in focus from self-protection to altruism, with the wearing of a mouth-and-nose guard increasingly becoming a symbol of mutual consideration and cohesion in the context of the pandemic (Cheng et al., 2020).

Taken together, the results imply that wearing a mouth-and-nose guard not only protects the wearer from COVID-19 and, through the perceived level of self-protection, also increases the sense of cohesion and thereby equally improves psychological well-being (Szczesniak et al., 2020).

5.4.4   The Paradox of Self-Defeating Prophecy in the Context of the COVID-19 Pandemic

Often incorrectly referred to in the media as the paradox of prevention or prevention paradox, a paradoxical effect occurred in the context of the COVID-19 pandemic, which is correctly referred to as a self-defeating prophecy, i.e. the opposite of a self-fulfilling prophecy. A self-defeating prophecy triggers reactions due to its feared occurrence, so that it does not come true.

Specifically, the consequence of this self-defeating prophecy was that, due to the great effectiveness of the measures taken to contain the COVID-19 pandemic in terms of its spread or dangerousness, many people after the first wave gained the impression that this disease was less contagious or dangerous than generally assumed.

The behavioural consequence of this collective misjudgement was that many people, after the decline in the number of cases, treated the recommended preventive measures carelessly, so that the emergence of a second wave and third wave was favoured or accelerated.

In summary, this momentous, almost collective misperception is a cognitive bias (systematic distortion of perception), which should be countered above all by appropriate risk communication and education.

5.5   Risk Factors for Mental Stress

Risk factors for psychological distress in general include female gender, younger age ($\leq$40 years), presence of chronic physical or psychiatric illness, unemployment, student status, and frequent consumption of social media or media reports related to COVID-19, according to a meta-study that analyzed data from 93,569 individuals studied (Xiong et al., 2020).

The following sociodemographic factors were also more strongly associated with depression or anxiety: Living alone, lower educational level, but also higher education, student status, not having a child, or having more than two children (Vindegaard & Benros, 2020).

5.6   Risk Groups

In principle, there is a strong consensus as to which groups of people are at greater risk of experiencing adverse mental health consequences. While at the beginning of the pandemic the focus was on health care workers, people with pre-existing mental health conditions, people with acute or chronic health problems and older people, the circle of those potentially at risk has widened.

The following groups of people were subsequently identified: Children and adolescents as well as people who suffered due to extra workload (especially women) or economic consequences (unemployed) as well as people with problematic substance use behaviour (especially alcohol) and people with existing addictions.

5.7   Resilience Factors in the Period of COVID-19

The resilience factors shown to be effective in the context of the COVID-19 pandemic include an optimistic attitude, the use of social support and the maintenance of social ties. They also include reduced media consumption and the development of strategies for relaxation and distraction.

Also of importance is to seek experiencing joyful moments, being able to laugh and reducing social isolation through online communication. At the family level, resilience factors such as flexibility, good family cohesion, appropriate communication with each other and financial management adapted to the situation have been identified (Chen & Bonanno, 2020).

5.8   Resilience in the Post-Pandemic Phase

Using the experience of past crises or disasters as a guide, researchers found that an estimated 10% of people will develop severe mental health problems such as anxiety disorders, depression, or post-traumatic stress disorder (PTSD) as a result of the current pandemic.

Current research suggests that many people have developed a COVID-19 stress syndrome during the current pandemic, characterized by fear of infection, fear of touching surfaces or objects that may be contaminated with the COVID-19 virus. Other effects noted include COVID-19 related safety behaviors and traumatic COVID-19 related stress symptoms (e.g. intrusive thoughts and nightmares).

Research on resilience suggests that two-thirds of people will be able to withstand the stresses of COVID-19. Some of these people will experience new meaning and purpose in their lives, for example, by helping others during the pandemic or pursuing new ways of living.

Nevertheless, according to many experts, there is reason to be concerned that there may not be sufficient mental health resources to support or treat the large numbers of people who are suffering psychologically as a result of the pandemic (Taylor & Asmundson, 2020).

Conclusion

- The most common adverse mental health consequences of the COVID-19 pandemic are stress, anxiety, and depression.
- Some effective nonpharmaceutical interventions (isolation, quarantine) to combat the pandemic may have adverse consequences for the human psyche that need to be mitigated. For this reason, it is essential that sufficient resources are allocated to the mental health of the population during but also after the pandemic phase in order to minimise the damage to society and the economy.
- At-risk groups or people who have risk factors can mitigate adverse consequences by adopting resilience-promoting behaviours. This fact and the necessary knowledge about it should be communicated to as many people as possible.

Social Aspects of the COVID-19 Pandemic

6

The range of individual and societal reactions is so broad that only selected and to date sufficiently researched psychosocial aspects of the COVID-19 pandemic are listed and briefly described below without claiming to be exhaustive. Further aspects can be found on the companion website to the book at www.mindster.at/covid-19-and-psychology.

6.1 Alternative and Pseudo-Medical Recommendations

Alternative and pseudo-medical recommendations for the prevention, detection or treatment of a COVID-19 infection have spread massively since the end of January 2020, both in the traditional media and in social media. It was observed that the nature of the recommendations was strongly adapted to the respective challenges of the pandemic phase and increased in number, variety and radicality as the duration progressed.

One of the world's best-known recommendations for detecting COVID-19 disease, which was circulated as a chain letter from the beginning of March 2020, was the advice to check whether one was already ill by holding one's breath for 30 seconds. This was combined with the advice to drink water every 15 minutes to prevent the virus from adhering to the mucous membrane.

As a result, the range of supposed remedies for the prevention or treatment of COVID-19 expanded rapidly. In order of appearance, five phases of pseudo-medical recommendations could be identified.

Alternative And Pseudo-Medical Recommendations And Their Development
First, these were "proven" natural remedies (garlic, vinegar, onion, ginger, beer, urine from animals), as well as the use of homeopathics.

© Springer Fachmedien Wiesbaden GmbH, part of Springer Nature 2021
J. G. Haas, *COVID-19 and Psychology*, essentials,
https://doi.org/10.1007/978-3-658-34893-9_6

Secondly, it was the use of dietary supplements as well as CBD (cannabidiol) and UV rays. The consumption of disinfectants or whole body rubs with them were also recommended at this stage.

Thirdly, the recommendation of (potentially) harmful substances such as colloidal silver, cocaine, ethyl or methyl alcohol, hydrogen peroxide, chlorine dioxide and MMS (solution of 28% sodium chlorite and 10% citric acid), as well as ventilation with oxyhydrogen gas, became rampant.

Fourthly, the recommended "off-label" use of substances such as hydroxychloroquine (antimalarial), aspirin, and acetaminophen was noted.

Fifthly, these were electronic devices ("coronavirus electrolyzer") as well as amulets, magic symbols or spiritual (distant) healing.

The dangers of pseudo-medical advice are not only its ineffectiveness, but above all its possible harmfulness, whereby the consequences can reach up to death.

Example Of A Pseudo-Medical Recommendation With A Fatal Outcome
Sad notoriety was achieved in April 2020 by a rapidly spreading recommendation in Iran to consume toxic methyl alcohol, which was conservatively estimated to have resulted in several hundred deaths (Hassanian-Moghaddam et al., 2020).

6.2   Loneliness

Human beings are social creatures by nature and therefore have a fundamental need to belong. If this need is not fulfilled, feelings such as loneliness, perceived undesirability, subjective worthlessness or a sense of inner emptiness can arise. As a result, these have an impact on well-being or on an existing mental disorder.

The severity of the consequences is directly related to the extent of subjectively perceived loneliness and depends on the individual assessment (Heinrich & Gullone, 2006). However, since loneliness is in principle a major risk factor for anxiety disorders and depression, it should naturally be kept small (Palgi et al., 2020).

6.3 Rumors

Rumors are forms of social exchange. They promote social cohesion by fostering the establishment and maintenance of relationships, the conveyance of a favourable impression to the counterpart and, last but not least, the agreement on a common knowledge or action. (Fig. 6.1.) As a rule, increased rumors are the reaction to ambiguous facts that are difficult for the individual to interpret. Particularly in this context, rumors can have a sense-making effect because they attempt to satisfactorily explain cases of luck, misfortune as well as coincidence and fate (Fine, 2005).

Rumors—Between Useful And Harmful
From an evolutionary psychological point of view, rumors fulfill the role of "survival legends" that offer orientation to individuals by attempting to channel reservations, prejudices, moods, desires, fears, and hopes. However, rumors also mean that they cannot be well distinguished from facts because of their apparently high plausibility and can lead to a polarisation of opinions and the consolidation of prejudices, thus threatening social consensus. The rapid spread of an increasingly large number of rumors in recent decades has been facilitated above all by digital forms of communication.

In the context of COVID-19, too, rumors and speculation fuelled public and media discourse and were devoted to the emergence, social and health consequences, prevention and cure of the disease, of which, according to one study, around 80% turned out to be untrue or inaccurate. Compared with other pandemics, rumors about the alleged violent consequences of the pandemic proved to be particularly high (Islam et al., 2020).

> ↪ Forwarded
> Ladies and gentlemen, I think you know me well enough to know,that I am not prone to to rash or panicky actions. I may suggest that to you as well. Nevertheless, I have it on good authority that there will be massive disruptions to the Austrian infrastructure very soon, possibly before the weekend.
> It is therefore recommended, that you all fill up your cars with gas and stock up on basic foodstuffs for a few DAYS. I do not mean hoarding purchases for the next few weeks!!!
> The basic supply (supermarkets etc.) will remain in any case. I ask again, do not fall into panic. There is no reason for it. Remain as prudent as before and use the small time advantage.
> 19:13

Fig. 6.1 Chain letter with warning that circulated in Austria 3 days before the first "lockdown", which effectively took place on March 13th of 2020. (From the author's archive)

6.4   Society and Popular Culture

Duden, the German-language spelling dictionary, fulfills a contemporary role by including and deleting terms. In August 2020, for example, it became known that several COVID-19-related terms such as "face mask", "herd immunity", "lockdown", "reproduction number" and "social distancing" have now already found their way into the 28th edition of the Duden.

From the end of March 2020, popular culture references dedicated to the supposed prediction of COVID-19 began to accumulate on social media. First and foremost, the 1981 novel "The Eyes of Darkness" by US author Dean Koontz and a compilation of scenes from the TV series "The Simpsons" were discussed extensively worldwide, which ultimately promoted conspiracy theory views in particular.

6.5   Violence

6.5.1   Violence in Public Spaces

The non-systematic observation of worldwide reports allows the conclusion that certain forms of violence are favoured by the spread of the pandemic. However, this finding should be regarded as preliminary, as media coverage also focused on acts of violence in the context of demonstrations, conflicts between citizens (in the context of the mandatory masking or lockdown), and violence against things. This includes, for example, the destruction of 5G masts in some countries, which some people saw as the trigger for the pandemic.

6.5.2   Family and Sexual Violence

Since the social distancing and mass quarantine ('lockdown') measures came into force, several studies have consistently reported a sharp increase in the number of calls to help lines. Although no reliable figures are currently available, there is concern that the reported increased number of calls to help hotlines is also reflected in an increased number of domestic violence and abuse offences (Hiscott et al., 2020). Initial reports from authorities in western countries currently indicate only a slight increase or even initial reduction in offences of this type.

Based on the experience of past pandemics, official bodies and initiatives express concern that the number of cases of (sexual) abuse as well as the dissemination of child pornography could be on the rise and urge vigilance in this regard.

6.6   Crime

In the synopsis of official reports and reporting on crime, the following can be seen in western countries: offences related to the physical proximity (pickpocketing) or absence of people (burglary) are on the decline. With regard to homicides, the reports are inconspicuous.

"Virtual" crime, i.e. cybercrime and white-collar crime, is on the increase, with officials stressing that criminal individuals and organisations have reacted quickly to the changed circumstances. Furthermore, as in the case of past pandemics, the effect is that people's distress and uncertainty are abused for criminal activities.

Criminal activity in the field of cybercrime can be divided into four areas:

Forms Of Cybercrime During The COVID-19 Pandemic

- Online extortion in the form of blackmail emails or by means of malware.
- Online fraud with pharmaceutical products, alleged remedies, personal protective equipment or disinfectants in the form of product piracy, counterfeits or bogus offers. This can also include fraudulent calls to elderly people by supposedly distressed relatives.
- Credit offers with intent to harm, especially for businesses.
- Organized online crime that focuses on money laundering.

Internationally, criminal authorities agree that the focus is increasingly shifting from the bright field (crimes on record) to the dark field, which makes it more difficult to estimate the number of crimes and to punish them.

6.7   Media Coverage

An examination of the nature of headlines from 25 reputable English-language global media outlets during the period January to June 2020 found that the vast majority of all news stories had a negative emotional tinge. Specifically, 52%

of all headlines were designed to evoke negative emotions, while 30% evoked positive emotions and 18% were neutral.

Fear, confidence, anticipation, sadness and anger were identified in descending order as the predominant emotions in the headlines. Furthermore, the study came to the conclusion that the proportion of emotionally negative content in the reporting increased continuously with the continuation of the pandemic.

The study authors are also concerned that the media-generated sentiment may also have negative effects on people's well-being and on the mood of the economy (Aslam et al., 2020).

6.8   Panic Buying

In hindsight usually described as unfounded and exaggerated, panic buying and other measures of overprovisioning occur more frequently in times of crisis. The reason for this lies on the one hand in the fear of a shortage and on the other hand in a perceived loss of control, which is joined by the observation of other people's behaviour, which fuels the spiral of panic buying.

Even when the supply situation is good, panic buying can lead to negative short-term effects in terms of availability and subsequently actually cause a short-term shortage (Arafat et al., 2020). Even for people not involved in panic buying, media coverage and a possible shortage can promote the perception of a crisis that has now occurred.

6.9   Paranoid Thoughts

According to recent research, paranoid thoughts occur regularly in one third of the general population. A higher level of paranoid thoughts was found especially in people whose coping style can be described as either emotional, less rational, avoidant, and less distanced from problems. Furthermore, individuals with thoughts of these exhibited negative attitudes toward open expression of emotion and compliant behaviour while having lower socioeconomic status (Freeman et al., 2005).

Susceptibility to paranoid thoughts is highly correlated with belief in conspiracy theories, such that they fall on fertile ground in more people than usual during times of heightened stress. This is underlined by a recent study in the context of the pandemic, which concludes that the intolerance of uncertainty combined with paranoid thoughts favours the development of conspiracy thinking (Larsen et al., 2020).

6.10   Responses to Measures to Contain COVID-19

6.10.1 Willingness to Comply with Measures

In terms of willingness to voluntarily self-isolate, people with higher health anxiety show more willingness to comply with recommendations and orders from public agencies (Asmundson et al., 2020).

6.10.2 Criticism, Dissatisfaction and Resistance to Measures

From the observation of the media, it can be concluded that governmental measures to contain COVID-19 were supported by a large number of people at the beginning of the pandemic. Subsequently, criticism and dissatisfaction increased and found expression in the form of protests and demonstrations, among other things.

Since the end of March 2020, first protests and demonstrations took place in Western countries against governmental measures to contain COVID-19 ("lockdown", "mandatory masking", …). A brief analysis by the author with Google Trends showed that the two preliminary peaks of these events were noticeable in mid-April and late August 2020.

As of October 2020, two trends are noticeable: first, that the content of the protest moved away from health issues and became more diverse. Secondly, the composition of the participants has become more heterogeneous and includes proponents from a wide range of ideological and political groups, some of which contradict each other in terms of content.

6.11   Assigning Blame

Crisis situations have always fostered prejudice and hostility, which can also lead to concrete accusations of guilt. The background to this is that the occurrence of subjectively insufficiently explainable phenomena (illness, catastrophes, …) is loaded with social significance in the sense of coping. The resulting explanations of guilt and responsibility for the occurrence of this phenomenon reflect current social stereotypes, fears and prejudices and can be understood as social reactions of defense.

Defining causes of illness, for example, in this way provides an opportunity to protect existing social norms or relations by defining boundaries of "normal" behaviour that appear to be threatened. Through these attributions of blame, people attempt to create order and restore control over perceived threats or maintain existing social structures (Nelkin & Gilman, 1988).

The phenomenon of blame can now be described as a global one, as blame in the context of the COVID-19 pandemic, especially in social media, is widespread and on the rise worldwide. The range of attributions extends from minorities to governments, politicians, institutions, NGOs and celebrities.

6.12   Social Support and Cohesion

Social support, i.e. helpful interaction with other people to cope with a problem, can take the form of recognition, attention, comfort and encouragement, but also practical help or the provision of information.

Based on Le Bon's influential work "The Crowd: A Study of the Popular Mind" (1895), which described human behaviour in crisis situations as impulsive, irrational and antisocial, more recent findings show the opposite. In contrast, current empirical studies in the context of epidemics and pandemics report only low levels of collective panic, but also of cohesion and social behaviour during such a crisis.

It can be said that both individual and societal responses to threats are primarily of a bonding nature. Because the presence of a common external threat such as a pandemic strengthens social bonds, contemporary society seems to be far from structural breakdown, according to research (Dezecache, 2015). In the context of the COVID-19 pandemic, the multitude of spontaneous expressions of cohesion, as well as the large number of initiatives and the use of volunteers in all countries, testify to this in many ways.

6.13   Stigmatisation

An existing uncertainty and fear lead not only in pandemic times to an effect called social stigmatization, which can be described as a label of social undesirability due to a certain characteristic. In the context of the pandemic, this is the characteristic of being a possible carrier of infection and concerns persons or groups who are either ill with COVID-19, are at risk of contracting it or are suspected of having contracted it.

As a result of this effect, they are shunned, treated unfairly, or in extreme exceptional cases attacked. The effect of stigmatization has been observed and described for both infectious and other diseases since the beginning of medical history.

In the course of the COVID-19 pandemic, ethnic groups (people from the Asian region, but also others), older people as well as suspected cases, convalescents, refugees, young people and people with mental or physical illness were victims of stigmatisation. Last but not least, people in health care professions should be mentioned, especially as they are exposed to a massive burden in the combination of strong occupational stress and social stigmatisation.

In addition to the psychological suffering that occurs in people affected by stigmatisation, these people may also have the effect of delaying or not seeking clarification of their complaints or treatment at all, thus increasing the risk of death and contributing to a more rapid spread of the disease.

6.14   Suicide Attempts and Suicide

There are findings from the SARS epidemic (2003) and the Spanish flu (1918–1919) that there is a connection between an increased rate of attempted and completed suicides and an epidemic or pandemic. The authors of this study blame this primarily on a lack of social cohesion and prolonged fear (Sher, 2020).

Another study from April 2020 lists a number of risk factors for suicide risk associated with COVID-19. These are financial stressors, domestic violence, alcohol use, loneliness, grief, limited access to food, and irresponsible media reporting, in addition to an existing mental health disorder (Gunnell et al., 2020).

A study dedicated to identifying suicide-related search queries on Google in the US concluded that the risk of suicide tended to be lower in the short term, but could increase in the long term (Halford et al., 2020).

In principle, most of the authors on this topic, as well as the WHO, explicitly point out that the prevention of suicide in times of pandemic should be an urgent social goal and emphasize in this context the important role of help hotlines and general practitioners (early detection).

6.15   Conspiracy Theories

Due to the controversial nature of conspiracy theories and the increasing irreconcilability with which representatives and critics confront each other, there is an increasing danger that constructive discourse will be rendered impossible, which usually begins with the definition of the term.

A common definition is that a conspiracy theory is characterized by the belief that a group of actors are conspiring in secret to achieve a hidden goal that is perceived as unlawful or malicious (Butter, 2020, p. 96).

Conspiracy Thinking As An Expression Of Subjective Disadvantage
From a social psychological point of view, it seems worth mentioning that among an increasing number of people there is a need for closed and well-explained narratives, which in many cases manifests itself in conspiracy-theory thinking.

On closer examination, this style of thinking is often accompanied by the subjective feeling of alienation, powerlessness, hostility and disadvantage. For this reason, from a humanistic point of view, the social goal of accommodation should be the creation of thriving social and economic conditions. The consequence of this is that more people can once again feel a sense of acceptance, efficacy and cohesion.

Disparagement can also lead some people to see not only their worldview, but also their person as disparaged or even threatened.

An April 2020 review of COVID-19 pandemic conspiracy theories circulating worldwide revealed, in aggregate, four narrative strands

Conspiracy Theories Circulating Worldwide About The COVID-19 Pandemic

- The virus as related to the 5G network, explaining the Chinese provenance of the virus through the connection to the communications giant Huawei
- The release, either accidental or deliberate of the virus from, alternately, a Chinese laboratory or an unspecified military laboratory, and its role as a bio-weapon
- The perpetration of a hoax by a globalist cabal in which the virus is no more dangerous than a mild flu or the common cold
- The use of the pandemic as a covert operation supported by Bill Gates to develop a global surveillance regime facilitated by widespread vaccination

From the study authors' point of view, these conspiracy theories also seem to combine in sequence and eventually form a single grand explanation that encompasses all of these actors.

It is not only here that we can see that the narrative intention of conspiracy theories is to show rejection by a small, overpowering out-group, ultimately to increase the cohesion of the in-group along the lines of "them or us". One of the great dangers is that such narratives primarily favour two options, one being to retreat into helplessness and the other to prevent the perceived evil—with all its negative consequences for society.

Like almost all other conspiracy theories, these also defy any rational and argumentative treatment and present people with the choice of believing or not believing them.

6.16 Insecurity

From a systems theory perspective, it can be stated that the social fabric is a highly complex system. In this context, complex means that both the amount of available information and the number of decision-making and action options have increased massively in the recent century. For this reason, people are increasingly required to make a concrete choice from the abundance of options available.

The resulting paradox is that with the freedom that has arisen comes an equally great uncertainty. This uncertainty is further amplified in times of crisis by the large amount of newly available information and opportunities.

Since, from an evolutionary perspective, humans tend to reduce uncertainty in principle and especially in times of stress, the subjective sense of control and efficacy is reduced, which fosters increased anxiety.

6.17 Perceived Social Consensus

A Pew Research Center study released in August 2020 of more than 14,000 people surveyed in 14 countries (including the U.S., Canada, France, Spain, Italy, and Germany) concluded that an average of 73% (88% in Germany) of respondents said that coping with the COVID-19 pandemic had gone well.

However, the pandemic has had a divisive effect on feelings of social unity in many of the countries surveyed: a median of 46% feel more united today than before the outbreak of the pandemic, while 48% feel that social division has increased. This finding includes 77% of Americans who say they are more divided than before the pandemic, while only 18% believe the country is more united.

6.18   Perceived Change in Living Conditions

An August 2020 Pew Research Center study reports that globally, a median of 58% report that their lives have changed significantly or greatly due to COVID-19. Women, in particular, have indicated that they have felt the changes brought about by the pandemic particularly strongly.

6.19   Xenophobia and Racism

Xenophobia and racism have always been more prevalent during pandemics and manifest themselves in mistrust, avoidance and accusation of people perceived differently. On several occasions these phenomena have reached exorbitant proportions, culminating in the persecution and murder of people. Not only, but primarily in the time of the plague in the Middle Ages, outbreaks of disease became the reason for the persecution of Jews and later also of other groups of people.

While at the beginning of the COVID-19 pandemic it was people from the Asian cultural area (media naming of the SARS-CoV-2 virus as "China virus", "Wuhan virus") who experienced xenophobia and racism, the focus shifted to People of Color (PoC) or indigenous people in US America and later to ethnic minorities in other countries as the cases of the disease spread worldwide.

As of August 2020, the online encyclopedia Wikipedia lists racist incidents in the context of COVID-19 in 46 countries on all continents. As the pandemic progressed, forms of discrimination, defamation or threats against groups of people developed that were independent of the region of spread, targeting people of Jewish or Islamic faith as well as homosexual and transsexual people, but also religious minorities.

Conclusion

- During the COVID-19 pandemic, a wide range of experiences and behaviours occur that can, in principle, be seen as the result of human coping efforts.
- Within this spectrum, both individually and socially beneficial and, in some cases, massively detrimental effects can be observed.
- Compared to previous pandemics, the role of (social) media and the rapidly spreading fear, as well as the increased occurrence of conspiracy theories, but also the stronger cohesion is particularly striking.

"Harmful Information"—Causes and Consequences of an Infodemic

"We're not just fighting an epidemic; we're fighting an infodemic" WHO Director-General Dr. Tedros Adhanom Ghebreyesus (2020)

The term infodemic, a cross between the terms information and epidemiology, was coined in 2000 by Gunter Eysenbach, a German health scientist. In his publication "Infodemiology: the epidemiology of (mis)information", he stated that much of the health information on the Internet can be described as inconsistent with information from evidence-based sources and therefore proposed criteria for testing the evidence-based nature of medical information (Eysenbach, 2002).

The World Health Organization classifies the potential impact of an infodemic as critical and now defines it as follows.

How an infodemic is defined
An infodemic is an overabundance of information—some accurate and some not—that makes it hard for people to find trustworthy sources and reliable guidance when they need it. […] It includes deliberate attempts to disseminate wrong information to undermine the public health response and advance alternative agendas of groups or individuals.

7.1 What Promotes an Infodemic and Why it is Dangerous

A 2018 RAND Corporation publication lamented the steadily diminishing role of factual knowledge in the American public sphere. This development is underpinned by the emergence of four interrelated trends (Kavanagh & Rich, 2018):

© Springer Fachmedien Wiesbaden GmbH, part of Springer Nature 2021
J. G. Haas, *COVID-19 and Psychology*, essentials,
https://doi.org/10.1007/978-3-658-34893-9_7

Four Main Trends That Promote An Infodemic

1. Increasing disagreement about facts and analytical interpretations of facts and data.
2. A blurring of the line between opinion and fact.
3. The increasing relative volume, and resulting influence, of opinion and personal experience over fact.
4. Declining trust in formerly respected sources of factual information.

The authors of the publication "Truth decay: an initial exploration of the diminishing role of facts and analysis in American public life" describe the drivers, mediators and consequences and their interrelationships as follows, thereby illustrating social contexts whose effects were also evident in the context of the COVID-19 pandemic. (Fig. 7.1.)

Assuming that the content nature of search queries and the frequency of occurrence of search terms reflect socially relevant interests, it seems necessary to monitor and moderate an infodemic, according to the judgment of these and other authors (Kavanagh & Rich, 2018).

Example Of Concrete Impact Of An Infodemic For example, a study devoted to global Google queries and Instagram hashtags in the period from late February to early May 2020 identified the following terms as the most frequently mentioned in the context of COVID-19: Ozone, lab, 5G, conspiracy, Bill Gates, milk, military and UV (Rovetta & Bhagavathula, 2020).

With regard to the relevance of an infodemic to society as a whole, the WHO states that it can have serious health effects because it is difficult for many people to find precise, evidence-based information and recommendations on their own health. Subsequently, this paves the way for both physical and mental illness.

In addition, an infodemic can cause people to believe misleading or dangerous advice. Last but not least, a general lack of interest or rejection of health-related content in general can also be the result.

The World Health Organisation also explicitly warns that certain content may also encourage xenophobia, hatred and exclusion.

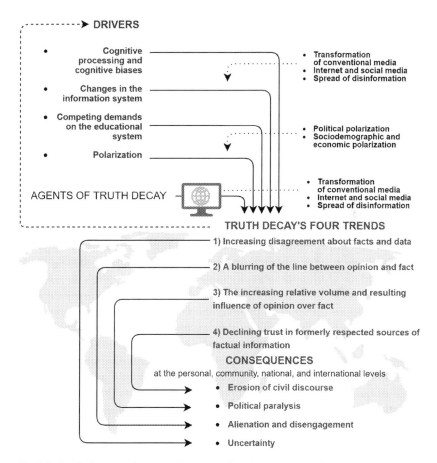

Fig. 7.1   Truth decay—drivers, mediators, trends and consequences in the representation of the RAND corporation

7.2   Infodemiology—How to Address an Infodemic Situation

Over the last few years, the societal relevance of infodemics has become increasingly urgent, leading the World Health Organization to convene the 1st WHO InfodemiologyInfodemiology Conference in the context of the COVID-19 pandemic. At the event, which was held from June 30 to July 16, 2020, the WHO expressed its concern about current developments, proposed concrete measures to counter them and described the newly revived discipline of infodemiology as the "science of infodemic containment".

The World Health Organization recognizes that an infodemic cannot be prevented, but it can be moderated. To respond effectively to an infodemic, it calls for evidence-based interventions involving all relevant research disciplines to more rapidly identify misinformation and disinformation.

The German infodemiologyinfodemiology pioneer Eysenbach proposes the following measures to improve the management of infodemics and refers to them as the four pillars of infodemic management.

The Four Pillars Of Infodemie Management

- information monitoring (infoveillance),
- building eHealth literacy and science literacy capacity,
- encouraging knowledge refinement and quality improvement processes such as fact checking and peer review,
- accurate and timely knowledge translation, minimizing distorting factors such as political or commercial influences.

Conclusion

- Inaccurate, false or misleading health information has increased greatly over the last two decades and explosively during the time of the COVID-19 pandemic (infodemic).
- The oversupply and unreliability of health information poses massive risks to human health and can also encourage behaviours that lead to the adverse treatment of fellow human beings.
- For these reasons, the World Health Organization wants to raise public awareness and is trying to take action to fight an infodemic (infodemiology).

Coping Successfully with the COVID-19 Pandemic from a Psychological Perspective

8

In the context of the COVID-19 pandemic, WHO published a guide for adults and a guide for children aiming at strengthening individuals psychological resilience. Both guides address mental health coping and provide evidence-based advice for the general population in plain language (World Health Organisation, 2020).

8.1   The WHO Guide for Adults

This guide was published in March 2020 and focused on mitigating the effects of isolation and quarantine, emphasizing the aspect of mutual support as well as mindfulness of the body and psyche (Fig. 8.1.).

8.2   The WHO Guide for Children and Adolescents

The guide for children which also published in March 2020, aims to counter the changes experienced in the living environment with increased attention, the maintenance of routines and age-appropriate information. (Fig. 8.2.)

8.3   "Be Kind to Your Mind"—A Brief Guide by the CDC

In 2020, the Centers for Disease Control and Prevention (CDC) guide, which has now been prominently positioned on the first page of results for every COVID-19-related search query in Google. This measure plays a key role in ensuring that people in need of information are accurately provided with relevant information and advice.

© Springer Fachmedien Wiesbaden GmbH, part of Springer Nature 2021
J. G. Haas, *COVID-19 and Psychology*, essentials,
https://doi.org/10.1007/978-3-658-34893-9_8

It is normal to feel sad, stressed, confused, scared or angry during a crisis. Talking to people you trust can help. Contact your friends and family.

If you must stay at home, maintain a healthy lifestyle - including proper diet, sleep, exercise and social contacts with loved ones at home and by email and phone with other family and friends.

Don't use smoking, alcohol or other drugs to deal with your emotions. If you feel overwhelmed, talk to a health worker or counsellor. Have a plan, where to go to and how to seek help for physical and mental health needs if required.

Get the facts. Gather information that will help you accurately determine your risk so that you can take reasonable precautions. Find a credible source you can trust such as WHO website or, a local or state public health agency.

Limit worry and agitation by lessening the time you and your family spend watching or listening to media coverage that you perceive as upsetting.

Draw on skills you have used in the past that have helped you to manage previous life's adversities and use those skills to help you manage your emotions during the challenging time of this outbreak.

Fig. 8.1   WHO guide for adults: Coping with stress during the 2019-nCoV outbreak

Beginning with simple tips for stress reduction, this guide emphasizes the role of social exchange and the importance of "rituals" for the body and psyche, and urges patience with oneself in a time of uncertainty. (Fig. 8.3.)

Children may respond to stress in different ways such as being more clingy, anxious, withdrawing, angry or agitated, bedwetting etc. Respond to your child's reactions in a supportive way, listen to their concerns and give them extra love and attention.

Children need adults' love and attention during difficult times. Give them extra time and attention. Remember to listen to your children, speak kindly and reasure them. If possible, make opportunities for the child to play and relax.

Try and keep children close to their parents and family and avoid separating children and their caregivers to the extent possible. If separation occurs (e.g. hospitalization) ensure regular contact (e.g. via phone) and re-assurance.

Keep to regular routines and schedules as much as possible, or help create new ones in a new environment, including school/learning as well as time for safely playing and relaxing.

Provide facts about what has happened, explain what is going on now and give them clear information about how to reduce their risk of being infected by the disease in words that they can understand depending on their age.

This also includes providing information about what could happen in a re-assuring way (e.g. a family member and/or the child may start not feeling well and may have to go to the hospital for some time so doctors can help them feel better).

Fig. 8.2   WHO guide for children: Helping children cope with stress during the 2019-nCoV outbreak

8.4   Overall Societal Management of the COVID-19 Pandemic

"It's easy to blame someone, it's easy to politicize, it's harder to tackle a problem together and find solutions together." WHO Director-General Dr Tedros Adhanom Ghebreyesus (2020)

Be kind to your mind
From cdc.gov

Mental health problems are common. Here are ways to cope with stress and promote wellbeing.

🌿   Pause. Breathe. Notice how you feel.   ∧

Take slow deep breaths, stretch, or meditate.

Observe how you are feeling and what you are thinking, without judgment. Instead of responding or reacting to those thoughts or feelings, note them, and then let them go.

🖼   Take breaks from upsetting content   ∧

Make time to unwind. Try relaxation techniques and listening to music. Try to do some other activities you enjoy.

🧍   Take care of your body   ∧

Exercise regularly. Even one session of moderate-to-vigorous physical activity reduces anxiety, and even short bouts of physical activity are beneficial.

Physical activity basics

Get plenty of sleep. Be consistent. Go to bed at the same time each night and get up at the same time each morning, including on the weekends.

Tips for better sleep

Try to eat healthy, well-balanced meals. Add healthy fats, cut sodium, bump up your fiber, and aim for a variety of colors on your plate.

Healthy eating tips

Avoid alcohol and drugs.

👥   Reach out and stay connected   ∧

Talk with people you trust about your concerns and how you are feeling.

Check in with your loved ones often. It can help you and your loved ones feel less lonely and isolated.

📞   Seek help if overwhelmed or unsafe   ∧

If you, or someone you care about, are feeling overwhelmed with emotions like sadness, depression, or anxiety, or feel like you want to harm yourself or others, seek professional help.

If distress impacts activities of your daily life for several days or weeks, talk to a clergy member, counselor, or healthcare provider.

For informational purposes only. Consult your local medical authority for advice.

Fig. 8.3 CDC guide "Be kind to your mind" on Google

Finally, if we look at the situation in society as a whole, the global outcome of the fight against the COVID-19 pandemic can be described as the result of overcoming all psychological, social and economic risk factors through the available resilience factors at the same levels (Fig. 8.4.).

Last but not the least, the important role of appreciation of fellow human beings should be emphasized in this way, as this forms the basis of a cooperative and successful pandemic response.

Conclusion

- Official guides to mental health in times of pandemic include understandable and easy-to-follow advice that has been shown to be highly effective when followed consistently.
- The successful management of a pandemic is more dependent on psychological factors than most people realize.
- The outcome of the COVID-19 pandemic can be viewed, simply put, as the result of mitigating risk through the whole-of-society resilience.

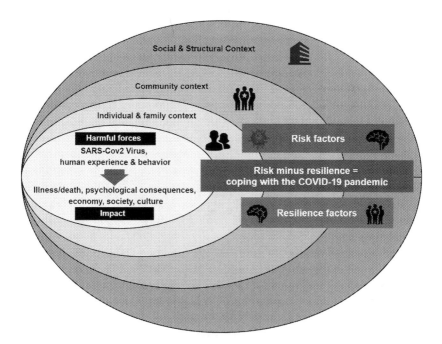

Fig. 8.4 Overall societal management of the COVID-19 pandemic from a systems theory perspective

What You Learned f rom This *essential*

- Infectious diseases have been with us since the beginning of time and have always posed major challenges.
- Epidemics and pandemics have their roots in human behaviour,
- In times of great stress, such as during a pandemic, people try to adapt in a variety of ways, although some forms of adaptation can have detrimental consequences for the individual and society.
- Successful management of a pandemic must be holistic and take into account psychological and social factors in the form of collective action, otherwise the cohesion of society as a whole may be threatened.

© Springer Fachmedien Wiesbaden GmbH, part of Springer Nature 2021
J. G. Haas, *COVID-19 and Psychology,* essentials,
https://doi.org/10.1007/978-3-658-34893-9

Bibliography

Aberth, J. (2005). *The black death.* Palgrave Macmillan US. https://www.doi.org/10.1007/978-1-137-10349-9.

American Psychiatric Association. (2013). *Diagnostic and statistical manual of mental disorders* (5th ed.). https://doi.org/10.1176/appi.books.9780890425596.

Arafat, S. M. Y., Kar, S. K., Marthoenis, M., Sharma, P., Hoque Apu, E., & Kabir, R. (2020). Psychological underpinning of panic buying during pandemic (COVID-19). *Psychiatry Research, 289.* https://doi.org/10.1016/j.psychres.2020.113061.

Aslam, F., Awan, T. M., Syed, J. H., Kashif, A., & Parveen, M. (2020). Sentiments and emotions evoked by news headlines of coronavirus disease (COVID-19) outbreak. *Humanities and Social Sciences Communications, 7*(1), 23. https://doi.org/10.1057/s41599-020-0523-3.

Asmundson, G. J. G., Paluszek, M. M., Landry, C. A., Rachor, G. S., McKay, D., & Taylor, S. (2020). Do pre-existing anxietyrelated and mood disorders differentially impact COVID-19 stress responses and coping? *Journal of Anxiety Disorders, 74.* https://doi.org/10.1016/j.janxdis.2020.102271.

Brooks, S. K., Webster, R. K., Smith, L. E., Woodland, L., Wessely, S., Greenberg, N., & Rubin, G. J. (2020). The psychological impact of quarantine and how to reduce it: Rapid review of the evidence. *The Lancet, 395*(10227), 912–920. https://doi.org/10.1016/S0140-6736(20)30460-8.

Butter, M. (Hrsg). (2020). *Routledge handbook of conspiracy theories.* Routledge.

Chen, S., & Bonanno, G. A. (2020). Psychological adjustment during the global outbreak of COVID-19: A resilience perspective. *Psychological Trauma: Theory, Research, Practice, and Policy, 12*(S1), S51–S54. https://doi.org/10.1037/tra0000685.

Cheng, K. K., Lam, T. H., & Leung, C. C. (2020). Wearing face masks in the community during the COVID-19 pandemic: Altruism and solidarity. *The Lancet, 0*(0). https://doi.org/10.1016/S0140-6736(20)30918-1.

Dezecache, G. (2015). Human collective reactions to threat. *Wiley Interdisciplinary Reviews: Cognitive Science, 6*(3), 209–219. https://doi.org/10.1002/wcs.1344.

Eysenbach, G. (2002). Infodemiology: The epidemiology of (Mis)information. *The American Journal of Medicine, 113*(9), 763–765. https://doi.org/10.1016/S0002-9343(02)01473-0.

Fine, G. A. (Hrsg.). (2005). *Rumor mills: The social impact of rumor and legend.* Aldine Transaction.

© Springer Fachmedien Wiesbaden GmbH, part of Springer Nature 2021
J. G. Haas, *COVID-19 and Psychology,* essentials,
https://doi.org/10.1007/978-3-658-34893-9

Freeman, D., Garety, P. A., Bebbington, P. E., Smith, B., Rollinson, R., Fowler, D., Kuipers, E., Ray, K., & Dunn, G. (2005). Psychological investigation of the structure of paranoia in a non-clinical population. *British Journal of Psychiatry, 186*(5), 427–435. https://doi. org/10.1192/bjp.186.5.427.

Gunnell, D., Appleby, L., Arensman, E., Hawton, K., John, A., Kapur, N., Khan, M., O'Connor, R. C., Pirkis, J., Appleby, L., Arensman, E., Caine, E. D., Chan, L. F., Chang, S.-S., Chen, Y.-Y., Christensen, H., Dandona, R., Eddleston, M., Erlangsen, A., ... & Yip, P. S. (2020). Suicide risk and prevention during the COVID-19 pandemic. *The Lancet Psychiatry, 7*(6), 468–471. https://doi.org/10.1016/S2215-0366(20)30171-1.

Halford, E. A., Lake, A. M., & Gould, M. S. (2020). Google searches for suicide and suicide risk factors in the early stages of the COVID-19 pandemic. *PLoS ONE, 15*(7). https://doi. org/10.1371/journal.pone.0236777.

Hassanian-Moghaddam, H., Zamani, N., Kolahi, A.-A., McDonald, R., & Hovda, K. E. (2020). Double trouble: Methanol outbreak in the wake of the COVID-19 pandemic in Iran— A cross-sectional assessment. *Critical Care, 24*(1), 402. https://doi.org/10.1186/s13054-020-03140-w.

Haug, N., Geyrhofer, L., Londei, A., Dervic, E., Desvars-Larrive, A., Loreto, V., Pinior, B., Thurner, S., & Klimek, P. (2020). Ranking the effectiveness of worldwide COVID-19 government interventions [Preprint]. *Epidemiology.* https://doi.org/10.1101/2020.07.06. 20147199.

Heinrich, L. M., & Gullone, E. (2006). The clinical significance of loneliness: A literature review. *Clinical Psychology Review, 26*(6), 695–718. https://doi.org/10.1016/j.cpr.2006. 04.002.

Hiscott, J., Alexandridi, M., Muscolini, M., Tassone, E., Palermo, E., Soultsioti, M., & Zevini, A. (2020). The global impact of the coronavirus pandemic. *Cytokine & Growth Factor Reviews, 53*, 1–9. https://doi.org/10.1016/j.cytogfr.2020.05.010.

Imran, N., Aamer, I., Sharif, M. I., Bodla, Z. H., & Naveed, S. (2020). Psychological burden of quarantine in children and adolescents: A rapid systematic review and proposed solutions. *Pakistan Journal of Medical Sciences, 36*(5). https://doi.org/10.12669/pjms.36.5.3088.

Islam, M. S., Sarkar, T., Khan, S. H., Mostofa Kamal, A.-H., Hasan, S. M. M., Kabir, A., Yeasmin, D., Islam, M. A., Amin Chowdhury, K. I., Anwar, K. S., Chughtai, A. A., & Seale, H. (2020). Covid-19–related infodemic and its impact on public health: A global social media analysis. *The American Journal of Tropical Medicine and Hygiene.* https:// doi.org/10.4269/ajtmh.20-0812.

Kar S. K., Yasir Arafat S. M., Kabir R., Sharma P., Saxena S. K. (2020) Coping with mental health challenges during COVID-19. In Saxena S. (eds) Coronavirus Disease 2019 (COVID-19). *Medical Virology: From Pathogenesis to Disease Control.* Springer, Singapore. https://doi.org/10.1007/978-981-15-4814-7_16.

Kavanagh, J., & Rich, M. (2018). Truth decay: An initial exploration of the diminishing role of facts and analysis in american public life. *RAND Corporation.* https://doi.org/10.7249/ RR2314.

Kim, S.-W., & Su, K.-P. (2020). Using psychoneuroimmunity against COVID-19. *Brain, Behavior, and Immunity, 87*, 4–5. https://doi.org/10.1016/j.bbi.2020.03.025.

Kramer, A. D. I., Guillory, J. E., & Hancock, J. T. (2014). Experimental evidence of massive-scale emotional contagion through social networks. *Proceedings of the National Academy of Sciences, 111*(24), 8788–8790. https://doi.org/10.1073/pnas.1320040111.

Larsen, E. M., Donaldson, K., & Mohanty, A. (2020). *Conspiratorial thinking during COVID-19: The roles of paranoia, delusionproneness, and intolerance to uncertainty* [Preprint]. PsyArXiv. https://osf.io/mb65f.

Milman, E., Lee, S. A., & Neimeyer, R. A. (2020). Social isolation as a means of reducing dysfunctional coronavirus anxiety and increasing psychoneuroimmunity. *Brain, Behavior, and Immunity, 87*, 138–139. https://doi.org/10.1016/j.bbi.2020.05.007.

Morens, D. M., Folkers, G. K., & Fauci, A. S. (2008). Emerging infections: A perpetual challenge. *The Lancet Infectious Diseases, 8*(11), 710–719. https://doi.org/10.1016/S1473-3099(08)70256-1.

Morens, D. M., Folkers, G. K., & Fauci, A. S. (2009). What is a pandemic? *The Journal of Infectious Diseases, 200*(7), 1018–1021. https://doi.org/10.1086/644537.

Nelkin, D., & Gilman, S. L. (1988). Placing blame for devastating disease. *Social Research, 55*(3), 361–378.

Oosterhoff, B., Palmer, C., Wilson, J., & Shook, N. (2020). *Adolescents' motivations to engage in social distancing during the covid-19 pandemic: Associations with mental and social health* [Preprint]. PsyArXiv. https://osf.io/jd2kq.

Palgi, Y., Shrira, A., Ring, L., Bodner, E., Avidor, S., Bergman, Y., Cohen-Fridel, S., Keisari, S., & Hoffman, Y. (2020). The loneliness pandemic: Loneliness and other concomitants of depression, anxiety and their comorbidity during the COVID-19 outbreak. *Journal of Affective Disorders, 275*, 109–111. https://doi.org/10.1016/j.jad.2020.06.036.

Pappas, G., Kiriaze, I. J., Giannakis, P., & Falagas, M. E. (2009). Psychosocial consequences of infectious diseases. *Clinical Microbiology and Infection, 15*(8), 743–747. https://doi.org/10.1111/j.1469-0691.2009.02947.x.

Rovetta, A., & Bhagavathula, A. S. (2020). *Global infodemiology of covid-19: Focus on google web searches and instagram hashtags* [Preprint]. Public and Global Health. https://doi.org/10.1101/2020.05.21.20108910.

Salari, N., Hosseinian-Far, A., Jalali, R., Vaisi-Raygani, A., Rasoulpoor, S., Mohammadi, M., Rasoulpoor, S., & Khaledi-Paveh, B. (2020). Prevalence of stress, anxiety, depression among the general population during the COVID-19 pandemic: A systematic review and meta-analysis. *Globalization and Health, 16*(1), 57. https://doi.org/10.1186/s12992-020-00589-w.

Schaller, M., & Park, J. H. (2011). The behavioral immune system (And why it matters). *Current Directions in Psychological Science, 20*(2), 99–103. https://doi.org/10.1177/0963721411402596.

Shahsavari, S., Holur, P., Tangherlini, T. R., & Roychowdhury, V. (2020). *Conspiracy in the time of corona: Automatic detection of covid-19 conspiracy theories in social media and the news. arXiv:2004.13783 [cs].* https://arxiv.org/abs/2004.13783.

Sher, L. (2020). The impact of the COVID-19 pandemic on suicide rates. *QJM: An International Journal of Medicine*, hcaa202. https://doi.org/10.1093/qjmed/hcaa202.

Shultz, J. M., Cooper, J. L., Baingana, F., Oquendo, M. A., Espinel, Z., Althouse, B. M., Marcelin, L. H., Towers, S., Espinola, M., McCoy, C. B., Mazurik, L., Wainberg, M. L., Neria, Y., & Rechkemmer, A. (2016). The role of fear-related behaviors in the 2013–2016 west africa ebola virus disease outbreak. *Current Psychiatry Reports, 18*(11), 104. https://doi.org/10.1007/s11920-016-0741-y.

Szczesniak, D., Ciulkowicz, M., Maciaszek, J., Misiak, B., Luc, D., Wieczorek, T., Witecka, K.-F., & Rymaszewska, J. (2020). Psychopathological responses and face mask restrictions during the COVID-19 outbreak: Results from a nationwide survey. *Brain, Behavior, and Immunity, 87*, 161–162. https://doi.org/10.1016/j.bbi.2020.05.027.

Taylor, S., & Asmundson, G. J. G. (2020). Life in a post-pandemic world: What to expect of anxiety-related conditions and their treatment. *Journal of Anxiety Disorders, 72*, https://doi.org/10.1016/j.janxdis.2020.102231.

Thucydides, S. R. B., & Crawley, R. (2008). *The landmark Thucydides: A comprehensive guide to the Peloponnesian War.* Free Press.

Tomes, N. (2000). The making of a germ panic, then and now. *American Journal of Public Health, 90*(2), 191–198. https://doi.org/10.2105/AJPH.90.2.191.

Vindegaard, N., & Benros, M. E. (2020). COVID-19 pandemic and mental health consequences: Systematic review of the current evidence. *Brain, Behavior, and Immunity, S0889159120309545*, https://doi.org/10.1016/j.bbi.2020.05.048.

Wellcome Collection. (n.Y.). Wilson „The plague...": people fleeing from plague. Retrieved 15. August 2020, from https://wellcomecollection.org/works/wuhtpjqa.

Werner, C., & Langenmayr, A. (2005). *Das Unbewusste und die Abwehrmechanismen.* Vandenhoeck & Ruprecht.

Wittchen, H.-U., & Hoyer, J. (Hrsg.). (2011). *Klinische Psychologie & Psychotherapie* (2., überarbeitete und erweiterte Auflage). Springer.

World Health Organisation. (2020). Mental health and COVID-19. Retrieved 15. August 2020, from https://www.who.int/teams/mental-health-and-substance-use/covid-19.

Xiong, J., Lipsitz, O., Nasri, F., Lui, L. M. W., Gill, H., Phan, L., Chen-Li, D., Iacobucci, M., Ho, R., Majeed, A., & McIntyre, R. S. (2020). Impact of COVID-19 pandemic on mental health in the general population: A systematic review. *Journal of Affective Disorders, 277*, 55–64. https://doi.org/10.1016/j.jad.2020.08.001.

Read More

Butter, M. (Hrsg.). (2020). *Routledge handbook of conspiracy theories.* Routledge.

Fine, G. A. (Hrsg.). (2005). *Rumor mills: The social impact of rumor and legend.* Aldine Transaction.

Hays, J. N. (2005). *Epidemics and pandemics: Their impacts on human history.* ABC-CLIO.

HHuremović, D. (2019). *Psychiatry of pandemics: A mental health response to infection outbreak.* Springer. https://doi.org/10.1007/978-3-030-15346-5.

Jetten, J., Haslam, S. A., Reicher, S., & Cruwys, T. (Hrsg.). (2020). *Together apart: The psychology of COVID-19.* SAGE Publications.

Kucharski, A. (2020). *The rules of contagion: Why things spread - and why they stop.*

Taylor, S. (2019). *The psychology of pandemics: Preparing for the next global outbreak of infectious disease.*

Companion Website to the Book

Due to the scope of this publication, only selected findings on the topic of COVID-19 and the psyche can be covered.

You will therefore find further content on the companion website to the book at www.min dster.at/covid-19-and-psychology, which will be updated at regular intervals.

Index

© Springer Fachmedien Wiesbaden GmbH, part of Springer Nature 2021
J. G. Haas, *COVID-19 and Psychology,* essentials,
https://doi.org/10.1007/978-3-658-34893-9

Printed in the United States
by Baker & Taylor Publisher Services